Brush up your French!
A revision guide for grown-ups

By Lucy Martin

Copyright © 2017 Lucy Martin
LMT Publications
London, United Kingdom

This book is dedicated to everyone out there who is brave enough to pick it up and have a go…

Contents **Page**

Getting started 5

Lesson 1	Le, la, les	11
Lesson 2	Possessive adjectives: mon, ma mes…	13
Lesson 3	Using "de"	15
Lesson 4	Activities	17
Lesson 5	Food, shopping and restaurants	21
Lesson 6	Using aller	25
Lesson 7	Weather	27
Lesson 8	Pain, doctors, hospitals	29
Lesson 9	Present tense regular verbs	32
Lesson 10	Present tense irregular verbs	34
Lesson 11	Past tense	38
Lesson 12	Imperfect tense	42
Lesson 13	Future tense	46
Lesson 14	Pronouns and other bits and pieces	49

Vocabulary and idioms 57

Getting started

You spent years at school learning French, and may have even reached a decent standard, so what a waste of all that time and effort if it all slides into disuse, leaving you only able to ask for a loaf of bread or a coffee. True, you don't *need* to speak French. But there is so much more fun to be had when you can communicate on a higher level than "où est la gare?". A holiday in France or any other French-speaking country (and there are 29 of them) is a much richer experience if you can establish contact other than with the waiter and the baker. Communication is what makes us human, makes us happy, and forms the bedrock of any functioning society; and yet with the advent of technology, hypermarkets, Google maps, all-inclusive hotels, the need for actual speech has all but disappeared.

So what stops us talking to the person at the next table in the cafe? It could be self-consciousness, fear of making mistakes, prejudice, laziness, being "too busy", or just letting real-life conversation slip down the list of priorities as we check our emails and expand our virtual network rather than any human one. The reality is that when you do open your mouth, you probably won't sound French, you will make mistakes, and they may smile and correct you, but they will love you for making the effort, and you will feel good. Getting out there and talking is like going to the gym. It's not an appealing thought, but make the effort to do it and you will be pleased you did.

In this book, although I have assumed a certain base level of knowledge, such as the fact that adjectives agree with nouns and mostly come after the noun, I have included plenty of language and grammar points you probably haven't used since school. But unlike a school text book, this one is designed to get you talking rather than reciting verbs and learning vocab, so I have included a series of dialogues showing conversations that you might have where you can practise what you have learnt. Each conversation is accompanied by a translation and a set of notes. This isn't a phrase book, it's more like a grammar book with a reminder of how, why and when to use each grammar point. For example, the whole point of knowing whether food is *du, de la* or *des*, is so that you can order in a restaurant or buy food in a shop. Rather than learning the set phrase *"je voudrais de la pizza avec des frites"*, isn't it more satisfying to understand, and have a magical way of remembering, which foods take which articles? I believe in finding those magical ways of remembering things, because no-one, least of all busy adults, has the time or the inclination to learn by rote. My vocabulary section at the back contains a wealth of memo techniques to give you crucial links between words and their meanings.

So, what are we waiting for? Let's get you back out there talking to French people about more than just the price of tomatoes.

Imagine you see a woman sitting on her own at a table outside the local café. She checks her phone, then puts it back in her handbag, takes a sip of coffee and smiles at you as you look around for somewhere to sit. Now you can just ignore her, or your day can take an unexpected turn, as you find yourself discussing international politics, and the problems of the youth of today, before embarking on some family fun and games on the beach, which leads to a lifelong friendship…

This includes some pretty advanced stuff, but this is what you're aiming for, not what you are expected to be able to do now, and everything in here will be explained. Enjoy!

DIALOGUE ONE

L : C'est libre?

MC: Oui c'est libre.

L : Bonjour, je m'appelle Lucy.

MC: Enchantée, Marie-Claude. Vous êtes en vacances?

L : Oui, nous sommes arrivés samedi, et vous? Vous êtes française?

MC: Oui mais je viens de Lille. Je suis en vacances comme vous, avec ma famille. Nous sommes arrivés mardi dernier.

L : *Première fois en Bretagne?*

MC: Non, la deuxième. Et vous?

L : *Je viens chaque année et je voudrais acheter une maison ici mais après le Brexit…*

MC: Ah oui, rien n'est certain. En France non plus.

L : *C'est vrai. Le monde est en train de changer.*

MC: Si seulement le temps était en train de changer. J'en ai marre.

L : *Oui on se croirait en Angleterre. Mais les enfants s'amusent à la plage quand-même. Ça ne les dérange pas, la pluie.*

MC: Tu as de la chance. Mes enfants sont accros à leurs portables et n'arrêtent pas de jouer aux jeux en ligne.

L : *C'est un problème chez les jeunes, pas comme quand j'étais jeune. Il n'y avait même pas d'ordinateur chez moi!*

MC: Chez moi non plus. Je me demande comment ils vont s'en sortir à l'avenir

L : *D'abord, ils auront des boulots qui n'ont pas encore été inventés.*

MC: Absolument, on ne doit pas s'inquiéter, mais ce que je trouve difficile, c'est le manque de conversation. On dirait qu'ils vivent dans un monde diffèrent.

L : *Il faut mettre en place des règles de base, on devrait les encourager à faire plus de sport.*

MC: Ah oui, on devrait jouer au cricket sur la plage, en famille.

L : *Bonne idée. Cet après-midi?*

MC: Les anglais contre les français, un match transmanche.

L : *A plus tard alors. Beau temps, mauvais temps.*

MC: D'accord. A tout-à-l'heure.

In case that was a struggle, here's a translation. Make a note of the expressions you didn't know. They might include *"j'en ai marre"* and *"à tout-a-l'heure", "s'en sortir"* and *"ce que"*, all of which are super-useful phrases if you are talking to or listening to French people.

TRANSLATION

Is this free?

Yes it's free.

Hello, my name's Lucy.

Pleasure to meet you. Marie Claude. Are you on holiday?

Yes we arrived Saturday. How about you? Are you French?

Yes but I come from Lille. I'm on holiday like you, with my family. We arrived last Tuesday.

First time in Brittany?

No, second. How about you?

I come every year and I would like to buy a house here but after Brexit….

Oh yes, nothing is certain in France either.

That's true, the world is changing.

If only the weather was changing. I'm sick of it.

Yes you'd think you were in England. But my kids still enjoy the beach. The rain doesn't bother them.

You're lucky. My kids are addicted to their phones and are constantly playing games online.

It is a problem with young people, not like when I was young. We didn't even have a computer.

8

Nor did we. I wonder how they are going to cope in the future. Firstly they will have jobs that haven't been invented yet.

Absolutely. There's no need to worry, but what I find hard is the lack of conversation. They seem to live in a different world.

You need ground rules, we should encourage them to do more sport.

Yes, we should be playing cricket on the beach as a family.

Good idea. This afternoon?

English v French, a cross-channel match!

See you later then, rain or shine.

Ok, see you later.

Text notes

1. Firstly, note the "**vous**" form. In French, until you are invited to do otherwise, call all other adults "vous" rather than "tu". Children can be called "tu". If you're not sure of the age, play safe and use "vous".

2. When asking questions, you can just make a statement and use a questioning voice "**c'est libre?**" rather than "est-ce que c'est libre?". You don't need to invert subject and verb as you were taught at school either. Say "vous êtes en vacances?" rather than " êtes-vous en vacances?"

3. Use "fois" for time, if you mean occasion, so "**une fois**" means "once" but "temps libre" means free time.

4. "**Chez**" normally means "at the house of" as in "chez nous" and "chez Gerard", but it can also mean "amongst", so "il y a beaucoup de depression chez les jeunes".

5. "**Rien n'est** certain" – The French for "nothing" is "rien" but it takes a negative verb, so it needs a "ne" before the verb. You

may have heard the croupier line in a casino "rien ne va plus" when no more bets can be placed. Similarly "personne" which means "nobody", takes a "ne" – personne ne mange les legumes" ("nobody is eating the vegetables").

6. Note the use of the indefinite pronoun "on". It can mean "one" in order to express what "one" must, should, can, or ought to do, or it can mean "we" as a direct replacement for "nous" and using simpler singular verb forms (eg: **"on devrait"** can mean "one ought to", and "we should").

7. **Modals** such as devoir (the infinitive from "on devrait") are followed by the infinitive. Using modal verbs and verbs of liking, preferring and disliking, you can completely avoid having to conjugate verbs :"On devrait les encourager"

8. Some other expressions take infinitives. "Le monde est **en train de** changer" means "the world is (in the middle of) changing". It's a good expression to use if you want to get across that something is actually going on now, because in French you don't have what we call the "present continuous" which allows us to distinguish between "I eat" and "I am eating" which are both "je mange" in French.

9. **"Ce que ..... c'est que"** is an extremely useful and easily translatable phrase meaning "what .... Is that". So to say "what I like is that there is lots to do" you say "ce que j'aime c'est qu'il y a beaucoup à faire."

10. Idioms to make a note of: **"j'en ai marre"** (I'm sick of it), and **"j'ai de la chance"** (I'm lucky). The expression **"s'en sortir"** meaning "to cope" is best learnt in phrases like "je ne sais pas comment je vais m'en sortir!" (I don't know how I'm going to cope).

11. The expression **"à tout-à-l'heure"** is a confusing one. They use it to say see you later, but then if you want to say that you met someone just a minute ago on the street, that would be "tout-a-l'heure" as well. So it means "in a while" and "a while ago" at the same time.

Lesson 1

"The" = le / la / les

Whenever you say "the" in English, then you're going to use *le / la / les* in French.

Le for masculine nouns   le chien = the dog

La for feminine nouns   la maison = the house

Les for plural nouns   les enfants = the children

AND

You use le / la / les before a noun is the subject of the verb that follows:

Les chiens sont sympas   Dogs are nice

Le chocolat est délicieux   Chocolate is delicious

AND

Use le / la / les when you talk about parts of your body:

J'ai les cheveux bruns   I have brown hair

Je me suis cassé la jambe   I broke my leg

AND

You use le / la / les after verbs of liking, prefering or hating

J'aime les chiens   I like dogs

J'adore la neige   I love snow

Je n'aime pas les documentaires I don't like documentaries

Lesson 2

Possessive adjectives: My, your, his, her, our, their

If it says "my" in English you need to say "my" in French.

Mon with masculine nouns   mon chien = my dog

Ma with feminine nouns   ma maison = my house

Mes with plural nouns   mes enfants = my children

This works with *your* (**ton, ta, tes**) and *his / her* (**son, sa, ses**) But "our", "your" and "their" only have singular and plural forms.

Notre chien / maison = our dog / house

Nos enfants = our children

Votre chien / maison = your dog / house

Vos enfants = your children

Leur chien / maison = their dog / house

Leurs enfants = their children

Practise definite articles and possessive adjectives

1. I like chocolate
2. He likes dogs
3. I like my cat
4. He likes his friends
5. They hate their teacher
6. I don't like wine
7. I hate meat
8. I prefer sweets
9. She doesn't like peas
10. Dogs are nice

Answers

1. I like chocolate — J'aime le chocolat
2. He likes dogs — Il aime les chiens
3. I like my cat — J'aime mon chat
4. He likes his friends — Il aime ses amis
5. They hate their teacher — Ils détestent leur prof
6. I don't like wine — Je n'aime pas le vin
7. I hate meat — Je déteste la viande
8. I prefer sweets — Je préfère les bonbons
9. She doesn't like peas — Elle n'aime pas les petits pois
10. Dogs are nice — Les chiens sont sympas

Lesson 3

Pas de, beaucoup de, plus de, moins de, trop de

"De" basically means "of". So if there is a lot of, too much of, too many of, more of, less of something then it's not a big surprise that you're going to use "de".

BUT the surprise is that if you ***don't*** have / eat / do something then that uses "de" as well.

Je n'ai pas d'argent	I don't have any money
Il n'y a pas de pistes cyclables	there aren't any cycle paths
Je ne mange pas de viande	I don't eat meat
Je ne fais pas de sport	I don't do sport
Il y a beaucoup de pain	there is a lot of bread
Il y a trop de chiens	there are too many dogs
Il y a plus d'enfants	there are more children
Il y a moins de pollution	there is less pollution

Practise these *(remembering that liking / disliking is followed by le / la / les – that rule comes first)*

1. I like French
2. I don't like snails
3. I don't have a cat
4. There isn't any noise
5. I don't eat meat
6. I don't like sport
7. I don't do sport
8. I don't have my passport
9. I don't have a passport
10. I don't have the time

Answers

1. *I like French* — J'aime le français
2. *I don't like snails* — Je n'aime pas les escargots
3. *I don't have a cat* — Je n'ai pas de chat
4. *There isn't any noise* — il n'y a pas de bruit
5. *I don't eat meat* — Je ne mange pas de viande
6. *I don't like sport* — Je n'aime pas le sport
7. *I don't do sport* — Je ne fais pas de sport
8. *I don't have my passport* — Je n'ai pas mon passeport
9. *I don't have a passport* — Je n'ai pas de passeport
10. *I don't have the time* — Je n'ai pas le temps (because it's "the")

Lesson 4

Activities

Talking about what you like doing, what you did and what you are going to do is a normal part of conversation, but the problem with French is that every time we want to say "I went swimming", or "I like playing tennis", we have to stop and think, because we are going to use different verbs, and put in articles and prepositions where in English they are not required.

1. General verbs

Sometimes an activity verb is simple.

- lire – **je lis le** journal   I read the paper
- regarder – **je regarde la** télé   I watch TV
- écouter – **j'écoute de la** musique I listen to music
- aller – **je vais au** cinéma   I go to the cinema

2. Jouer

To play is "jouer", but what follows depends on whether it's it a game that you play and can win. If so, say **"je joue au / aux"**

- Je joue **au** tennis
- Je joue **au** netball
- Je joue **au** basket
- Je joue **aux** cartes

If it's an instrument "je joue du / de la"

- Je joue du piano   ("du du du" goes the piano)
- Je joue de la guitare ("la la la" singing to the guitar)

3. Faire"

In English, we talk about "*going*" cycling, swimming, horseriding, sailing, diving, skiing, surfing etc but in French you have to say you <u>do</u> these things. You know the verb "faire" - it means "do" which sounds like "du" so that's easy to remember:

- **Je fais du** sport
- **Je fais du** vélo / du cyclisme (cycling)
- **Je fais du** VTT (mountain biking)
- **Je fais du** patinage (skating)
- **Je fais du** judo / karate
- **Je fais du** ski
- **Je fais du** footing / jogging
- **Je fais du** shopping

But some activities are feminine and take "faire de la" rather than "faire du". Here's how to remember them. Imagine you're in the sea swimming, windsurfing, diving and sailing, looking back at the beach you see people doing dancing, weightlifting and gymnastics on the sand

- **Je fais de la** natation (swimming)
- **Je fais de la** voile (sailing)
- **Je fais de la** planche à voile (windsurfing)
- **Je fais de la** plongée (diving)
- **Je fais de la** gymnastique (gymnastics)
- **Je fais de la** danse (dancing)

If the activity in question begins with a vowel, then it's different again. We can't say du or de la before a vowel so we say "je fais de l'". For example,

- **Je fais de l'**équitation (horseriding)
- **Je fais de l'**alpinisme (mountaineering)
- **Je fais de l'**athlétisme (athletics)
- **Je fais de l'**escalade (climbing)
- **Je fais de l'**escrime (fencing)

And if you do lots of them, use "je fais des"

- **Je fais des** randonnées (hikes)
- **Je fais des** promenades (walks)

DIALOGUE 2

MC: Alors, vous faites quoi normalement, pendant votre temps libre?

L: Ça dépend. En hiver, pendant mon temps libre, j'aime lire, regarder la télévision et aller au cinéma. Le soir, nous jouons aux cartes après le diner et mes enfants jouent du piano.

MC: Ah bon, c'est la même chose chez nous. Et en été vous faites plus au plein air?

L: Ah si seulement c'était aussi simple que ça. Le temps n'est pas fiable chez nous. Mais je dirais qu'en été, je fais plus de sport. J'adore faire du sport. Le week-end, je fais du vélo avec mes enfants et en semaine je vais au gymnase pour faire de la musculation. Et vous?

MC: De temps en temps je joue au tennis avec ma copine et quand nous avons le temps nous faisons des randonnées à la campagne. J'aime faire de la natation et de l'équitation mais je n'ai pas de cheval et la piscine est loin de chez moi.

TRANSLATION

So what do you normally do in your free time?

It depends. In winter, during my free time, I like reading, watching TV and going to the cinema. In the evening we play cards after dinner and my children play the piano.

Ah, it's the same here. And in summer, do you do more outdoor stuff?

If only it was as simple as that. The weather isn't reliable back home. But I'd say that in the summer I do more sport. I love doing sport. At the weekend, I go cycling with my children and in the week I go to the gym to do weight training. What about you?

Sometimes I play tennis with my friend and when we have the time we go hiking in the countryside. I like going swimming and horse-riding but I don't have a horse and the pool is a long way from my house.

Text notes

1. *As we found out in dialogue one, asking questions in French isn't half as bad as it was at school. Here there are more questions, and, surprisingly, you can say "**vous faites quoi?**" or "you do what?" without seeming rude.*

2. *Use "**pendant**" with periods of time rather than "**dans**", unless you want to say "in two weeks' time" which is "dans deux semaines". If you went to Spain last year for two weeks, that too needs to use "pendant" because you were there during that amount of time. "Je suis allee en Espagne pendant deux semaines". If you're going there for two weeks, then it's "pour".*

Lesson 5

Food, shopping and restaurants

As we have established, in English we can miss out articles altogether but in French we can't, and food is another example of this linguistic nightmare. We say "I ate chips" but in French you need to put something in before the word "frites".

The food I ate today is "un, une, du, de la, or des"

That's the rule that will stop you saying "*ce matin j'ai mangé les cereales*". Le / La / Les are not on the list and is not an option when it comes to talking about food unless, as we set out in Lesson 1, you are talking about food you like / dislike "*j'aime les tomates*" or it's the subject of a verb, "Je pense que *les tomates sont bons*" (I think tomatoes are nice).

It's the rule that will stop you saying "*j'ai mangé de pizza*". De is not on the list either and is not an option when it comes to talking about food unless, as set out in Lesson 2, you are talking about having lots, of, too much of, enough of, more of or less of something, or if you don't have any at all, "*je n'ai pas de tomates / j'ai beaucoup de tomates*".

So when it comes to eating food, not liking it, or quantifying how much you have of it, use the mantra. I'll say it again:

"The food I ate today is un, une, du, de la or des".

Before we go any further I want to tell you about my **red and yellow** food list:

confiture (jam), viande (meat), pizza, sauce, soupe, glace (ice-cream – think strawberry flavour), mayonnaise and moutarde (mustard).

To work out which word to use with which food – un, une, du, de la or des, just follow these rules:

Do you eat the **whole thing**? Then say   **un / une**   if not….

Is it plural? Do you eat **lots of them**? Then say   **des**   if not….

Is it on my **red /yellow list**?   Then say   **de la**   if not…

                                         Then say   **du**

Remember that some food may fit into two categories – so you can have AN ice cream as well as SOME ice cream, and the same goes for pizza and cake…

Du	De la Red and yellow	Des	Un / une
Pain Fromage Beurre Jambon Poisson Poulet	Glace Pizza Viande Confiture Sauce Soupe Moutarde Mayonnaise	Pommes de terre Frites Petits pois Carottes Pâtes Céréales Haricots verts	Glace Pizza Pomme Croissant Poire Hamburger tomate

Now see if you can make your own lists under du, de la, des, un/une

DIALOGUE THREE

MC: Salut Lucy, ça va?

L: Très bien merci Marie-Claude. Nous avons fait du VTT pendant cinq heures ce matin. Je suis complètement crevée.

MC: Je m'imagine! Et vous avez eu faim après tout ça?

L: Le mot est faible. Mon fils avait une faim de loup. Il a mangé du poulet avec des légumes, du pain, des pâtes et des petits pois. Et pour le dessert, de la glace et du gâteau.

MC: Et les autres?

L: Nous avons tous mangé plein de malbouffe, trop de sucre, et encore plus de pain qu'hier. J'ai mangé de la pizza avec des frites, suivi par du pain et du fromage. Pour le dessert j'ai pris une salade de fruits avec de la glace et des biscuits.

MC: C'est tres méchant. Il faut au moins goûter les spécialités de la région avant de partir.

L: Oui mais pour aujourd'hui ça va. Je n'en peux plus. Juste un petit café. Garçon! Un café s'il vous plait. Et, où sont les toilettes?

TRANSLATION

Hi Lucy how are you?

Very well thank you Marie-Claude, but we did 5 hours mountain biking this morning. I'm completely exhausted.

I can imagine. Were you hungry after all that?

That's putting it mildly. My son was starving. He ate chicken with vegetables, bread, pasta and peas. And for pudding, ice-cream and cake.

And the others?

We all ate loads of junk food, too much sugar and even more bread than yesterday. I ate pizza with chips followed by bread and cheese. For pudding I had a fruit salad with ice cream and biscuits.

Very naughty. You at least have to try the local specialities before you leave.

Yes but that's enough for today. I can't take any more. Just a coffee. Waiter, a coffee please, and where are the loos?

Text notes

1. Note the use of **"prendre"** with food. The French don't like to talk about "eating"; they prefer to "take" meals.

2. To say "before you leave" in French, it's best to say "before leaving" and use **"avant de" + infinitive**. This avoids all sorts of problems with sentence structure.

3. To say "after eating" you use the structure "after having eaten" which is **"après avoir mangé"**

4. "Un café" in France is small and black. If you want a latte, ask for "un grand crème".

5. Toilets are always plural!

Lesson 6

Using "aller"

In English, we say "to the" for all places in a town, eg. *"I went to the cinema"*. But in French, there are four ways of saying "to the". *"Je vais **au** cinéma / **à la** piscine / **aux** magasins / **à l'**eglise"*. Here's how to remember the rules:

Places in the town

The general rule is "**au**" or "**aux**" if the place is plural. (*Imagine going into town and being surprised at everything you see. Put "oh!" before every noun, or the equivalent in French, "au".*)

- Je vais au cinéma
- Je suis allé au restaurant
- Je vais aller au parc
- Je vais aux magasins

But the feminine places in the town, take "**à la**". Imagine a holiday – you go **to the bank** to get money, **to the library** to get some books, then you go **to the station** to get the train. On the holiday you go **to the beach and the pool**, then **to the post office** to send a postcard home. Voilà!

au	**à la**
parc	banque
restaurant	bibliothèque
cinéma	gare
musée	piscine
magasin	plage
centre commercial	poste
centre sportif	

If you're going to somewhere plural it's "**aux**"
Je vais aux magasins   I go to the shops

If the place begins with a vowel, it's **à l'**
Je vais **à l'***église*   *I go to church*

25

Transport - If it's got an **en**gine, it's **en**

En avion	by plane
En voiture	by car
En car	by coach
En train	by train
En bus	by bus
En bateau	by boat

No engine? That means using your legs – "ahhhh!"
à pied, à vélo   on foot, by bike

Going to other countries – en or au

You need an engine to get to another country. Most countries use "*en*" whether you are going to that country "*Je vais **en France** en train*" or you're in it "*Je suis en France*", because they are feminine.

NB Masculine countries which take "au" include Canada, Japon, Portugal, Brésil and with the USA, it's "aux Etats Unis"

Going to towns - à

You don't need an engine to go to a town. You can go on foot or by bike, "*Je suis allé à Londres à vélo*".

Le week-end dernier…

Je suis allé	…………………piscine ………………………..	voiture
Je suis allé	…………………France………………	vélo
Je suis allé	…………………bibliothèque ……………	Londres
Je suis allé	…………………restaurant …………	Soho
Je suis allé	…………………centre commercial …………….	bus
Je suis allé	…………………poste ……………	pied

Lesson 7

Weather

Imagine (you don't need to actually believe, just imagine) that God ("il") makes the weather – so when you say *"il fait beau"* = you think *"he makes beautiful"*.

If you want to say anything about the weather, stick to this rule and talk about *il fait* or *il a fait / il faisait*, followed by *beau, chaud, mauvais* or *froid*.

Il fait beau	the weather is good / bad
Il faisait beau	the weather was good (generally)
Il a fait beau	the weather was good (specific occasion)
Il fera beau	the weather will be good
Le soleil brille	the sun is shining
Il y a du brouillard / du vent	it's foggy / windy
Il y avait du brouillard	it was foggy
il neige	it's snowing
il neigeait	it was snowing
Il a neigé	it snowed
la neige	snow
il pleut	it's raining
il pleuvait	it was raining
il a plu	it rained
il pleuvra	it will rain
il gèle	it's icy
un orage / une tempête	a storm
des nuages	clouds
la pluie	rain

French weather forecast - La météo

Aujourd'hui, dans le nord de la France, il y a des orages. A Paris, il y a des nuages. Dans l'est de la France, il fait froid. Il fait 5 degrés et il y a aussi des nuages. Dans l'ouest de la France, en Bretagne, il pleut. Il y a des nuages, de la pluie et du vent. Il ne fait pas chaud, il fait 8 degrés. Dans le sud-ouest, il fait beau mais frais : 11 degrés. Dans le sud de la France, il y a du soleil, mais attention, dans le sud-est, il y a du vent. Les montagnes, maintenant : il fait beau sur le Massif Central. Sur les Pyrénées, il y a des nuages. Et dans les Alpes, il neige, il fait 0 degrés.

Text notes

1. *Note that in French the verb "faire" is used extensively in weather and is used to measure temperature as well. "Il fait 5 degrés."*

2. *"Dans" is used to denote the points of a compass "dans le nord" but is quite rarely used for "in". Other times "dans" is used are "dans deux semaines" (in two weeks' time) "dans ma famille / ville" (in my family / town), "dans les Alpes" and whenever you are physically inside something like a mode of transport "dans la voiture".*

Lesson 8

Pain, doctors and hospitals

Whereas in English, we name the part of the body and follow it with the word *hurts,* the French say that they *have badly at the* head / arm / tooth.

J'ai mal au dos	My back hurts
J'ai mal au bras	My arm hurts
J'ai mal à la tête	My head hurts
J'ai mal à la jambe	My leg hurts
J'ai mal à la dent	My tooth hurts
J'ai mal aux dents	My teeth hurt
Ça fait mal?	Does it hurt ?
Ça fait mal	It hurts
Je me suis cassé la jambe	I broke my leg
Je me suis cassé le bras	I broke my arm
J'ai dû aller à l'hopital	I had to go to hospital

DIALOGUE FOUR

MC: Lucy! Qu'est-ce qui s'est passé? Tu boites?

L: Ce n'est rien. C'est pas grave. Je suis tombée du vélo. C'est tout. Je n'ai pas fait attention.

MC: Ah non, je suis désolée. Ça doit faire mal!

L: Un peu mais je n'ai pas envie d'aller à l'hôpital.

MC: Je pourrais t'emmener, si tu veux.

L: Non, merci, on part demain, et ça va aller. Je dois rentrer à l'appartement.

MC: Tu veux que je te ramène?

L: Oui je veux bien, merci Marie-Claude!

MC: Pas de soucis. C'est le moins que je puisse faire.

TRANSLATION

Lucy! What happened? Are you limping?

It's nothing. It's not serious. I fell off the bike. That's all. I wasn't being careful.

Oh no, I'm sorry, it must hurt.

A bit but I don't want to go to hospital.

I could take you if you like.

No thanks. We are leaving tomorrow and it will be fine. I have to get back to the apartment.

Do you want a lift?

Yes please, thanks Marie-Claude.

No worries. It's the least I can do.

Text notes

1. Marie-Claude is now addressing Lucy as **"tu"**, presumably because sufficient time has passed and it has been decided to do the "tutoyer" thing. Sometimes this will be specifically requested "on peut se tutoyer" or it may just happen, but safer to let your French friend decide!

2. Having said you can make questions with intonated statements, we now come across an exception. There's only one way to ask "what happened?" and it's **"qu'est-ce qui s'est passé?"**

3. **"Ce n'est rien"** and "je n'ai pas fait attention" both show how you make a verb negative by putting the "ne" and the "pas" or "rien" either side of the verb.

4. *"**C'est pas grave**"* should technically be *"ce n'est pas grave"* but the French would never pronounce the "ne" in speech.

5. To take someone somewhere – *"**emmener**"* indicates you will be staying with the person, whereas *"amener"* or *"ramener"* for taking back, implies dropping them off. To give someone a lift home is simply *"ramener"*.

6. Asking someone if they want you do do something, is structured so you say *"do you want that I …."* So for example *"**tu veux que je** regarde le film?"* but beware – the verb is in the subjunctive, which sometimes looks like a normal present tense, but not always! See 8 below, and p.54 for more subjunctive expressions.

7. *"**Avoir envie de**"* is another avoir expression, to join *"j'ai faim"*, *"j'ai de la chance"* and *"j'en ai marre"*, this time meaning to feel like doing something.

8. *"Le moins que je puisse faire"* is an idiom that uses the subjunctive – a *"mood"* as opposed to a tense which is best learnt in phrases until you get the hang of it.

Lesson 9

Present Tense regular verbs

There are three main types of verb, ending in –er, -re and –ir.

The first column is *"easy"* (the endings **e / es / e** sounds like **"eeeasy"** when you say it all together).

The second column is *"so so difficult"* **(s s d)**.

The third column is the LAST so th**IS IS IT**.

The plural section is **ons ez ent** every time, except for the last column where your batteries are running out, you're slowing down and you're adding sleepy snoring sounds to it with the *"iss"*.

-er jouer – to play	-re répondre – to reply	-ir finir – to finish
je joue tu joues il/elle/on joue nous jouons vous jouez ils/elles jouent SIMILAR VERBS *ecouter – to listen* *habiter – to live* *manger – to eat* *parler – to speak* *regarder - to watch* *aimer – to like* *laver – to wash* *ranger – to tidy* *porter – to wear* *commencer – begin* *terminer – to finish* *bavarder – to chat* *travailler – to work* *voyager – to travel*	je réponds tu réponds il/elle/on répond nous répondons vous répondez ils/elles répondent SIMILAR VERBS *vendre – to sell* *descendre – to go down* *entendre – to hear*	je finis tu finis il/elle/on finit nous finissons vous finissez ils/elles finissent SIMILAR VERBS *vomir – to be sick* *choisir – to choose* *ralentir – slow down*

Fill in the gaps and check with previous page

-er jouer – to play	-re répondre – to reply	-ir finir – to finish
je jou tu jou il/elle/on jou nous jou vous jou ils/elles jou SIMILAR VERBS *ecouter –* *habiter –* *manger –* *parler –* *regarder -* *aimer –* *laver –* *ranger –* *porter –* *commencer –* *terminer –* *bavarder –* *travailler –* *voyager –*	je répond tu répond il/elle/on répond nous répond vous répond ils/elles répond SIMILAR VERBS *vendre –* *descendre –* *entendre –*	je fin tu fin il/elle/on fin nous fin vous fin ils/elles fin SIMILAR VERBS *vomir –* *choisir –* *ralentir –*

Lesson 10

Present tense irregular verbs

Notice the rhymes with the verbs in bold – then when you know one you'll remember the others more easily.

	savoir *know a fact*	connaitre *know a person*	faire *to do / make*	aller *to go*
Je	**sais**	**connais**	**fais**	**vais**
Tu	**sais**	**connais**	**fais**	vas
Il	**sait**	**connait**	**fait**	va
Nous	savons	connaissons	faisons	allons
Vous	savez	connaissez	faites	allez
Ils	savent	connaissent	**font**	**vont**

	devoir *to have to*	boire *to drink*	recevoir *to receive*
Je	**dois**	**bois**	**reçois**
Tu	**dois**	**bois**	**reçois**
Il	**doit**	**boit**	**reçoit**
Nous	devons	buvons	recevons
Vous	devez	buvez	recevez
Ils	doivent	boivent	reçoivent

	Vouloir *to want*	pouvoir *to be able to*
Je	**veux**	**peux**
Tu	**veux**	**peux**
Il	**veut**	**peut**
Nous	voulons	pouvons
Vous	voulez	pouvez
Ils	veulent	peuvent

Modals

DEVOIR, POUVOIR AND VOULOIR are called modal verbs, this means they can't be used on their own and **are always followed by another verb in the infinitive**.

Je dois partir	I have to leave
Je peux venir	I can come
Je veux bavarder	I want to chat

ALLER can either be used on its own:
Je vais au cinema   I go to the cinema
Or followed by another verb in the infinitive (future tense):
Je vais aller au cinema   I'm going to go to the cinema

SAVOIR can be used on its own:
Je sais / Je ne sais pas   I know / I don't know
Or with a noun:
Je sais la reponse   I know the answer
Or followed by another verb in the infinitve:
Je sais nager   I can swim (I know how to swim)

How do you say

1. I want
2. I drink
3. I must
4. I go
5. I do
6. He goes
7. We go
8. We can
9. They go
10. We do
11. He does
12. She does
13. He drinks
14. She drinks
15. We drink

Answers

1. *I want*   je veux
2. *I drink*   je bois
3. *I must*   je dois
4. *I go*   je vais
5. *I do*   je fais
6. *He goes*   il va
7. *We go*   nous allons
8. *We can*   nous pouvons
9. *They go*   ils vont
10. *We do*   nous faisons
11. *He does*   il fait
12. *She does*   elle fait
13. *He drinks*   il boit
14. *She drinks* elle boit
15. *We drink*   nous buvons

More Irregular verbs in family groups....

jeter / appeler to throw / call *(note the double letter)* Je jette / j'appelle Tu jettes / appelles Il jette / appelle Nous jetons / appelons Vous jetez / appelez Ils jettent / appellent	**de-/re- /venir / tenir** to become, come back, come, hold je viens tu viens il vient nous venons vous venez ils viennent	**com- / ap- / prendre** To understand, learn, take je prends tu prends il prend nous prenons vous prenez ils prennent
acheter to buy *(note the accent in 4/5)* j'achète tu achètes il achète nous achetons vous achetez ils achètent	**voir / croire** to see / believe *"seeing is believing!"* je vois / crois tu vois / crois il voit / croit voyons / croyons vous voyez / croyez ils voient / croient	**partir /sortir/dormir** to leave/go out/sleep *(what teenagers do)* je pars / sors / dors tu pars / sors / dors il part / sort / dort partons/sortons /dormons partez/sortez/dormez partent/sortent/dorment
dire / lire / conduire to say, read, drive Je dis / lis / conduis Tu dis / lis / conduis Il dit / lit / / conduit disons/lisons/conduisons dites / lisez / conduisez Ils disent / lisent / conduisent	**mettre / permettre** To put / permit Je mets Tu mets Il met Nous mettons Vous permettez Ils permettent	**(d)écrire** to write (describe) J'écris tu écris il écrit nous écrivons vous écrivez ils écrivent

Lesson 11

Past tense "passé composé"

The passé composé
begins with "je me suis", "je suis" and " j'ai"
The e is acute and the r goes away
You could begin it "le week-end dernier"

This tense is used to relate events that have happened and are over. You build it using a person and auxiliary verb, then add your verb in the past participle.

FIRST, CHOOSE A BEGINNING

There are three possible beginnings in the first person:

Je me suis (for verbs mainly to do with bedroom / bathroom) eg:

se réveiller (to wake up), se lever (to get up), se laver (to wash), se doucher (to shower), s'habiller (to get dressed), se brosser les dents (to clean your teeth) s'amuser (to have fun), se casser la jambe (to break your leg – falling off the bed?), se coucher (to go to bed)

Je suis ("house" verbs relating to the comings and goings in a house) eg:

aller (to go), venir (to come), arriver (to arrive), partir (to leave), entrer (to enter – see also "rentrer" to return or go back in), monter (to go up), descendre (to go down), tomber (to fall), mourir (to die), rester (to stay), naître (to be born) and retourner (to return)

J'ai (everything else) eg:

manger (to eat), regarder (to watch), écouter (to listen), jouer (to play), prendre (to take), faire (to make or do), dire (to say), voir (to see), devoir (to have to), pouvoir (to be able to), and many more…

SECOND, ADD A PAST PARTICPLE

After one of those beginnings, put the verb into past participle form.

The general rule is that er verbs change their ending to é, re verbs change theirs to u and ir verbs change theirs to i.

However, there are a number of exceptions…..

avoir	--> J'ai eu	I had
boire	--> J'ai bu	I drank
devoir -	--> J'ai dû	I had to
voir	--> J'ai vu	I saw
pouvoir	--> J'ai pu	I was able to
lire	--> J'ai lu	I read
venir	--> Je suis venu	I came
courir	--> J'ai couru	I ran
recevoir	--> J'ai reçu	I received
vivre	--> J'ai vecu	I lived
prendre -	--> J'ai pris	I took
comprendre	--> J'ai compris	I understood
mettre	--> J'ai mis	I put
dire	--> J'ai dit	I said
écrire	--> J'ai écrit	I wrote
ouvrir	--> J'ai ouvert	I opened
faire	--> J'ai fait	I did / made
être	--> J'ai été	I was
naitre	--> Je suis né	I was born
mourir	--> Il est mort	He died
pleuvoir	--> Il a plu	It rained

Past tense verb chart

Here is a chart showing which verbs go with which beginning, and all the verbs are in their correct past participle form. With the verbs that take être, the past participle must agree with the person in gender and number, hence the optional e and s. Fill in the gaps on the next page.

je me suis tu t'es il s'est elle s'est nous nous sommes vous vous êtes ils se sont elles se sont	*je suis* tu es il est elle est nous sommes vous êtes ils sont elles sont	*j'ai* tu as il a elle a nous avons vous avez ils ont elles ont
réveillé (-e) (-s)	allé (-e) (-s)	mangé, joué etc
levé (-e) (-s)	(re-) (de-) venu (-e)(-s)	répondu, vendu etc
lavé (-e) (-s)	(r) entré (-e) (-s)	fini
douché (-e) (-s)	sorti (-e) (-s)	fait
habillé (-e) (-s)	arrivé (-e) (-s)	été
couché (-e) (-s)	parti (-e) (-s)	eu
amusé (-e) (-s)	monté (-e) (-s)	bu, vu, lu, dû, pu, reçu, voulu, cru, su
	descendu (-e) (-s)	pris, compris, appris, mis
	tombé (-e) (-s)	ecrit, conduit, dit
	mort (-e) (-s)	
	resté (-e) (-s)	
	né (-e) (-s)	
	retourné (-e) (-s)	

je me suis *tu t'es* *il s'est* *elle s'est* *nous nous sommes* *vous vous êtes* *ils se sont* *elles se sont*	*je suis* *tu es* *il est* *elle est* *nous sommes* *vous êtes* *ils sont* *elles sont*	*j'ai* *tu as* *il a* *elle a* *nous avons* *vous avez* *ils ont* *elles ont*

Can you complete the chart with the past participles?

Lesson 12

Imperfect tense

This is used to describe

- an action in the past that was **repeated** (when I *was* young I *went swimming* every day, meaning I *used to*)

- or when you are stressing the fact that this **WAS going on** rather than the completion of the action (*I was cleaning* the house when the doorbell rang), but as mentioned earlier, you can achieve this by saying "j'étais en train de" – "I was in the middle of".

Common uses of the imperfect

C'était   it was

Il y avait   there was / there were

To make and use the imperfect tense...

Take the nous form of the present tense (eg **jouons**)

Take the ons off – and get **jou**... Then a*dd the endings*:

Je jou**ais**

tu jou**ais**

il jou**ait**

nous jou**ions**

vous jou**iez**

ils jou**aient**

The only exception to this rule is être – where you add the above endings on to "et" because there is no "ons" to take off in the nous form.

DIALOGUE FIVE

L: Allo?

MC: Salut Lucy! Tu vas bien?

L: Oui je bosse, depuis le retour, mais ça va. Et toi?

MC: Eh bien, je suis en train de faire la queue pour les vestiaires, et j'ai pensé à toi.

L: Les vestiaires? Où ça?

MC: Chez Zara, comme d'habitude. Oui je peux essayer ceux-ci? Merci

L: A ça y est alors? La queue va vite!

MC: Oui, enfin, et c'était comment, ton anniversaire?

L: Et bien, je voulais sortir au cinéma parce qu'il y avait un nouveau film que j'avais envie de voir. Mais mon mari ne voulait pas venir. Il voulait aller ailleurs. C'était une surprise et je ne savais pas, donc j'étais un peu fâchée qu'il ne voulait pas venir au cinéma.

MC: Ah non – dommage

Au restaurant il y avait trop de monde et on a dû aller chez Mcdo

MC: Tu plaisantes?

L: Oui, ne t'inquiètes pas! Il y avait un autre à côté. On a passé un bon moment. On a bu trop de vin, mais…

MC: Obligatoire!

L: Merci, mais aujourd'hui j'ai la gueule de bois…

MC: Repose-toi Lucy, tu le mérites!

L: Quand j'étais jeune je buvais beaucoup plus et je n'étais jamais malade, je sortais tous les soirs quand j'étais à la fac.

MC: me fais rire. C'est vrai. Moi aussi. Ça devient de plus en plus difficile de faire comme les jeunes!

TRANSLATION

Hello!

Hi Lucy, are you well?

Yes I've been working since I got back but it's okay, how about you?

Well I'm in a queue for the changing rooms, and I thought of you.

Changing rooms? Where?

At Zara, as usual. Yes, can I try these? Thank you.

So that's it then. The queue is moving fast!

Yes, at last, and how was your birthday?

Well I wanted to go to the cinema because there was a new film I wanted to see. But my husband didn't want to come. He wanted to go somewhere else. It was a surprise and I didn't know, so I was a bit cross that he didn't want to come to the cinema.

Oh no, what a shame.

At the restaurant there were too many people so we had to go to McDonalds.

You're joking?

Yes don't worry, there was another one next door. We had a good time. We drank too much wine but….

Of course!

Thanks, but today I am hungover.

Relax, Lucy, you deserve it.

When I was young I drank much more and I was never ill. I went out every night when I was at uni.

You make me laugh. It's true. Me too. It gets harder and harder to do what young people do!

Text notes

1. Here you can see the imperfect and passé composé used together. Verbs about wanting and knowing **"je savais" "je voulais"** are more commonly used in the imperfect because wanting and knowing isn't an actual event. It's more of a state.

2. **"Bosser"** is a common slang term for "travailler" and is used widely.

3. **"Depuis"** technically means "since" but be careful with tenses. Je joue au tennis depuis cinq ans" means "I've been playing tennis for 5 years." So if you want to express how long you have been doing something for, use the present tense with depuis.

4. To say "Where?" is a little feeble in French so they add "ça" on the end, as if to say "where's that then?" rather than just "où?" which can sound like a random noise.

5. We see here that **"chez"** can extend to shop names as well.

6. Lots of French expressions begin with "faire la…" so to queue is **"faire la queue"**, to party is **"faire la fête"**, to play the fool is "faire l'andouille".

7. Instead of saying "à l'université" try saying **"à la fac"** – it's much more common in France when talking about uni.

8. **"faire comme les jeunes"** means literally "to make like the young", in other words, do what young people do. A similar phrase is **"faites comme chez vous"** which means "make yourself at home."

Lesson 13

Future tense

1. "Zis is **je vais of ze future**"

My fake German accent has helped many a student remember that if we're in the future tense, we probably need to start with "je vais". *Zis is je vais of the future…*

You know the one – **je vais regarder la télé** / je vais aller au cinéma / je vais faire du sport. It's just like the English – I'm going to watch TV / go to the cinema etc. We use the present tense of the verb "to go" plus the infinitive, in both languages. This is the form of the future tense in most common use.

2. **My fAV tense**

The second type of future tense is my "fAV" tense because it's the Future (f) and it uses the endings from AVoir (AV), together making fAV. Hooray, no extra learning here because we know those endings are: **ai / as / a / ons / ez / ont**. For example: **je mangerai,** tu regarder**as**, nous écouter**ons**, ils prendr**ont**, il jouer**a**, vous trouver**ez**, elle prendr**a**

BUT some verbs have a different root – so we put those endings on something other than the usual infinitive. Here are the most important ones:

Etre	ser	Ce sera bien – it will be good
Avoir	aur	J'aurai fini – I will have finished
Faire	fer	Il fera chaud – it will be hot
Aller	ir	J'irai à pied – I will go on foot
Pouvoir	pourr	Je pourrai – I'll be able to
Devoir	devr	On devra – we'll have to

Put the imperfect endings on these to make the **conditional**: je serais = I would be.

DIALOGUE SIX – by email

MC: Salut Lucy, Ça va? Quels sont tes projets pour les vacances?

L: Salut MC, je ne sais pas encore les détails mais nous irons en Ecosse pour rendre visite à mes parents.

MC: Et vous allez faire quoi là?

L: Je vais me détendre, j'espère. Mon mari va jouer au golf, et mes enfants vont retrouver leurs amis.

MC: Tu reviendras en France, un jour?

L: Oui, en octobre, pour la Toussaint j'espère. Nous irons à Bordeaux, chez des amis qui viennent d'acheter des gites. Tu sais que tu es la bienvenue en Angleterre aussi ?

MC: Merci Lucy. Je viendrai l'année prochaine, quand j'aurai plus d'argent.

L: D'accord. A bientôt MC, désolée, je suis chargée et je dois m'en aller.

TRANSLATION

Hi Lucy. How are you? What are your plans for the holidays?

Hi MC, I don't know the details yet but we are going to go to Scotland to visit my parents.

And what are you going to do there?

I will relax, I hope. My husband will play golf and my children will meet up with their friends.

Will you come back to France one day?

Yes in October for half term I hope. We will go to Bordeaux to stay with some friends who have just bought some gites. You know you are welcome to come to England too?

Thanks Lucy. I will come next year when I have more money.

Ok. See you later MC, sorry I'm busy and I have to go.

Text notes

1. Sometimes the word "what" in English is translated by "**quel**" in French which means "which", so you say which are your plans, or which is your favourite animal / colour etc.

2. To talk about a visit to someone, as opposed to something, you can't use the verb "visiter". You need the expression "**rendre visite à**".

3. "**retrouver**" is a great word for "to meet up with".

4. Holidays in France are based around religious festivals, so October half term is called la **Toussaint**, after All Saints Day.

5. "**Venir de**" is used to express what you have just done. "I have just eaten" will be expressed as "I come from eating", or "je viens de manger".

6. To say someone is welcome – you say you are the welcomed one "**tu es le bienvenu** / la bienvenue" and when someone arrives, you might say "soyez la bienvenue".

7. Using "quand" (when) in the future, as in "when I get home" or "when I'm older", is a trigger for a future tense verb, so it's "**quand j'arriverai chez moi**" rather than "quand j'arrive chez moi".

8. "**S'en aller**" is a common reflexive verb, with the added complication of the "en", that the French use to mean go off somewhere, or leave. It's a bit stronger to say "je m'en vais" rather than just "je vais" or "je pars" which sound a bit half-hearted.

Lesson 14

Pronouns and other bits and pieces

In English we can put pronouns after verbs *"I like it" "he saw her", "they ate them"*

But in French you have to pop the pronoun in earlier *"je l'aime", "il la voit", "ils les mangent"* **BUT** you can avoid this completely by just repeating the noun *I like the film"* instead of *"I like it"*.

There are a few verbs that take indirect objects, such as donner, demander and dire, and these produce the same overall effect except in the third person where they change from le/la/les to *leur or leurs*.

Direct object pronoun *agrees with the noun it replaces!*	Indirect object pronoun with donner, dire, demander
Il me voit – he sees me	Il me donne - he gives me
Il te voit – he sees you	Il te donne - he gives you
Il **le** voit – he sees him	Il **lui** donne - he gives him/her
Il **la** voit – he sees her	
Il nous voit – he sees us	Il nous donne - he gives us
Il vous voit – he sees you	Il vous donne - he gives you
Il **les** voit - he sees them	Il **leur** donne - he gives them

These pronouns come before the verb in the present and past:

Il me voit
Je lui donne le livre
Il m'a vu
Je lui ai donné du pain

And between the two parts of the verb in the future tense:
Il va me voir
Elle va lui donner un café

You can put what is called a "disjunctive pronoun" after a preposition, as you can see in column three below. Here it's only nous and vous that stay the same

Disjunctive pronouns *used after a preposition*
avec **moi** – with me chez moi – at my house
avec **toi** - with you chez toi – at your house
avec **lui** - with him chez lui - at his house
avec **elle** – with her chez elle – at her house
avec **nous** – with us chez nous – at our house
avec **vous** – with you chez vous – at your house
avec **eux** – with them (m) chez eux – at their house
avec **elles** – with them (f) chez elles – at their house

Little words y and en

Put simply, "y" means "there" and "en" means "of it" and both words go before the verb in the sentence, and between the two parts of the verb in the future tense.

J'y vais – I go there

J'y suis allé – I went there

Je vais y aller – I'm going to go there

Tu en veux? – do you want some (of it)

These little words are used as substitutes, and whether you choose the y or the en depends on whether the verb you're using takes "à" "a" or "de". Where there is a verb that takes "à", like "aller" (to go – to) or "penser" (to think – about) then there will be an "y" to replace what follows and where there is a verb that takes "de", like manger (to eat) or faire (to do) there will be an "en".

Common verbs which use à

Aller   je vais à la banque – I go to the bank

j'y vais – I go there

Habiter   j'habite à Londres – I live in London

j'y habite – I live there

Penser   je pense à mes enfants – I'm thinking about my kids

j'y pense – I'm thinking about them

Verbs which take "de"

Manger   j'en mange – I'm eating some (of it)

Vouloir   j'en voudrais - I would like some (of it)

Faire   j'en fais – I do (some of) it

Relative pronouns qui and que – meaning which / that / who

Use **que** if the next word is a person or thing (think que …. je rhyme)

The book that I like – le livre **que** j'aime

The sport that I do – le sport **que** je fais

The food that I eat – la nourriture **que** je mange

Use **qui** if the next word is a verb

The book that is on the table – le livre **qui** est sur la table

The film that makes me laugh – le film **qui** me fait rire

Special verb structures

En lisant	while reading
Après avoir mangé	after eating
Avant de sortir	before going out
Je suis en train de	I'm in the middle of
Je viens de	I have just
Sur le point de	about to

Opinions and justifications

Je pense que	I think that
Je trouve que	I find that
Je le trouve facile	I find it easy
A mon avis	In my opinion
Selon moi	according to me
Parce que / car c'est	because it is

Positive opinions on things

Ça vaut la peine	it's worth it
Ça valait la peine	it was worth it
Ça fait du bien	it feels good
Ça me fait plaisir	it makes me happy
Je suis ravi de partir en vacances	I'm excited about my holiday
J'ai hâte d'y retourner	I can't wait to go back there
J'attends ……. avec impatience	I am looking forward to ……
On a passé un bon moment	we had a great time

C'est à tomber	it's to die for
Ça me fait rire	it makes me laugh

Negative opinions on things

J'en ai marre	I'm sick of it
J'en ai ras le bol	I've had enough
Ça me fait peur	I'm scared of it
C'est nul	It's rubbish
Je suis nul en maths	I'm rubbish at maths
J'ai horreur de	I have a horror of / hate
Un cauchemar	a nightmare

Avoir expressions

J'ai de la chance	I'm lucky
J'ai envie de	I want to, I feel like
J'ai du mal à	I find it hard to
J'ai hâte de	I'm looking forward to / can't wait to
J'ai besoin de	I need
Tout ce dont j'ai besoin	everything (of which) I (have) need

Comparatives and superlatives

Plus sympa que	nicer than
Moins sportif que	less sporty than
Le film le plus passionnant	the most exciting film
Le meilleur pays du monde	the best country in the world

Y and depuis

J'y habite depuis cinq ans	I've lived there for five years
J'y joue depuis cinq ans	I've been playing it for five years
J'ai envie d'y retourner	I'd like to go back there
J'y suis accro	I'm addicted to it
Je n'y suis jamais allé	I've never been there

En

Je m'en sers pour tout	I use it for everything
J'en profite	I make the most of it
J'en mange tous les jours	I eat it (some of it) evey day
Il n'y en a pas	There aren't any (cycle paths)
Il n'y en a pas assez	There aren't enough of them
Je ne pourrais pas m'en passer	I couldn't manage without it

Dont

Il y a tout ce dont j'ai besoin	There is everything I need
Le restaurant don't j'ai parlé	The restaurant I talked about

Preceding direct / indirect objects

Je le trouve ennuyeux	I find it boring
Ça ne lui dérange pas	It doesn't bother him
Je lui ai acheté un cadeau	I bought him / her a presesnt

Subjunctive expressions

Pour que je puisse	so that I can

Bien que ce soit	although it is
Quoi que ce soit	whatever it may be
Il faut qu'on fasse des efforts pour	we've got to try to
Avant que ce ne soit trop tard	before it's too late
Je ne pense pas que ce soit	I don't think it is

Impersonal expressions

On peut	one can / you can
On doit	one must / you have to
Il faut	you have to
Il me faut (plus time)	it takes me
Il me faut (plus noun)	I need
Il suffit de	all you have to do is
Il s'agit de	it's about

Negatives

Je ne fume pas	I don't smoke
Je n'ai jamais fume	I have never smoked
Je ne le ferai plus	I won't do it anymore
Personne ne fume	Nobody smokes
Il n'y a aucune raison	There is no reason
Il n'y a rien à faire	There's nothing to do
Il n'y a que des anglais	There are only English people

Ce que

Ce que j'aime le plus c'est	what I like best is
Ce que je n'aime pas, c'est que	what I don't like is that

Ce que je trouve bizarre, c'est	what I find strange is
Ce que trouve inquietant, c'est	what worries me is

Idioms and phrases that make you sound really French

Enchantée	Pleased to meet you
Bonne journée / soirée	Have a nice day/evening
Bonne continuation	Enjoy the rest of the holiday
A la prochaine!	See you next time!
J'en ai marre	I'm sick of it
J'en ai ras le bol	I've had enough
Ils ont du mal à se débrouiller	they struggle to get by
Il fait un froid de canard	it's freezing cold
Il pleut des cordes / à verse	it's pouring
Il n'arrête pas de faire l'andouille	he keeps messing about
Je n'en ferai pas une rame	I won't lift a finger
Ça coute les yeux de la tête	It costs a bomb
A vos souhaits	bless you!
Donner un coup de main à qq	to give someone a hand
Scotché à l'écran	glued to the screen
Le suspense m'a tenu en haleine	I was riveted
Ça ne m'a rien dit	It did nothing for me
C'etait vachement bien	It was really good
J'ai eu les yeux plus gros que le ventre	my eyes were bigger than my stomach

Vocabulary lists by topic

RELATIONSHIPS AND DESCRIBING PEOPLE
Family

dans ma famille	in my family
nous sommes quatre	there are 4 of us
mon père	my father
ma mère	my mother
mes parents	my parents
mon frère (ainé / cadet)	my older / younger brother
ma sœur (ainée / cadette)	my older / younger sister
mes grands-parents	my grandparents
mon cousin / ma cousine	my cousin
mon oncle	my uncle
ma tante	my aunt
Je suis enfant unique	I'm an only child
le bébé	baby
le mari	husband
la femme	wife / woman
le garçon	boy
Mon frère s'appelle	my brother is called
Je n'ai **pas de** sœur	I don't have a sister

How you get on – *use "on"!*

on s'entend bien	*we get on well*
beaucoup de choses en commun	*lots in common*
on se dispute	*we argue*

Adjectives to describe people

grand(e) / petit(e)	tall / small
gros(se) / mince	fat / thin
intéressant(e) / ennuyeux/-euse	interesting / boring
sympa / embêtant(e)	nice / annoying
vieux (vieille) / jeune	old / young
sportif/-ive / paresseux/-euse	sporty / lazy
gentil (gentille) / égoïste	kind / selfish
beau (belle), joli(e) / laid(e)	beautiful /pretty/ugly
fort(e) / faible	strong / weak
méchant(e) / sage	naughty / well-behaved
agréable / désagréable	pleasant / unpleasant
bavard(e) / silencieux /-ieuse	chatty / silent
marrant(e) / sérieux/-euse	funny / serious
poli(e) / impoli(e)	polite / impolite
triste / fâché(e) / heureux/-euse	sad / cross / happy
sensible / insensible	sensitive / insensitive
de bonne humeur	in a good mood
de mauvaise humeur	in a bad mood
fatigué / énergique	tired / energetic
prudent(e) / maladroit(e)	careful / clumsy
facile à vivre	easygoing
difficile	fussy

Hair adjectives – il a les cheveux….

longs / courts	long / short
raides	straight
frisés / bouclés	curly
blonds / roux / marron	blonde / red / brown
Il a les cheveux marron *(no s!)*	he has brown hair
Il est chauve	he is bald

General appearance

Il porte des lunettes	he wears glasses
une barbe	beard
une moustache	moustache
Je ressemble à ma mère	I look like my mother
On se ressemble	we look like each other

General adjectives

plein(e) / vide	full / empty
sain(e) / malsain(e)	healthy / unhealthy
facile / difficile	easy / difficult
chaud(e) / froid(e)	hot / cold
moderne / ancien (-ienne)	modern / old
individuel(le) / jumelé(e)	detached / semi-
cher / bon marché	expensive / cheap
payant / gratuit	payable / free
sec (sèche) / mouillé(e)	dry / wet
léger (légère) / lourd(e)	light / heavy
lent(e) / rapide	slow / fast

génial(e) / pénible	wonderful / awful
sale / propre	dirty / clean
nouveau / nouvelle	new
étroit(e) / large	narrow / wide

Half / step- and in-laws

This is where it gets complicated – demi can be step or half, and beau / belle can be step or in law – so best avoided!

mon demi-frère	my stepbrother or half brother
ma demi-sœur	my stepsister or half sister
ma belle-mère	my stepmother or mother-in-law
mon beau-père	my stepfather or father-in-law
mon beau-frère	my brother-in-law
ma belle-sœur	my sister-in-law

Types of relationship and family

toutes sortes de familles	all sorts of families
de bons rapports	good relations
une relation	a relationship
draguer	to chat up
petit copain	boyfriend
petite copine	girlfriend
un rendez-vous	a date
sortir avec	to go out with
tomber amoureux	to fall in love
l'amour	love
rencontrer	to meet
épouser	to marry

un couple	a couple
fidèle	faithful
ensemble	together (musical)
cohabiter	to live together
avant de se marier	before getting married
se marier avec	to marry
divorcé	divorced
marié	married
séparé	separated
une famille nombreuse	a big family
des familles recomposées	blended families
familles monoparentales	single parent families
le mariage gay	gay marriage
se disputer	to argue
plaquer	to dump (someone)
la valeur	value
la stabilité	stability
élever un enfant	to bring up a child
adopter	to adopt
les parents adoptifs	adoptive parents
la famille d'acceuil	adoptive family

Home

> **(Women own the house, car, road, the whole town…)**
>
> *Notice that all the rooms in the house, and a lot of the things around the house are **feminine** (house, door, window, car, shelves, wardrobe, TV). Imagine that the only place a man is allowed is the office, sitting room and garden. He can have a bed, a computer, a pen and a few other bits (see second list below) but he has to do the housework (le ménage).*

une maison individuelle	a detached house
une maison jumelée	a semi
une maison mitoyenne	a terraced house
une cuisine	a kitchen
une salle à manger	a dining room
une salle de bains	a bathroom
une chambre	a bedroom
une véranda	a conservatory
une voiture	a car
une table	a table
une armoire	a wardrobe *(reach arm in)*
une chaise	a chair
une porte	a door
une fenêtre	a window
une lampe	a lamp
une commode	a chest of drawers
une piscine	a swimming pool
une machine à laver	a washing machine

une cuisinière	a cooker
une télévision	a TV
une Xbox / Playstation	Xbox / Playstation
une ville	a town
une rue	a road

Picture a man in these rooms only

un salon	a sitting room
un jardin	a garden
un grenier	an attic
un bureau	an office

He can sit on

un canapé	a sofa
un fauteuil	an armchair
un lit	a bed

For entertainment he can have

un livre	a book
un ordinateur	a computer
un crayon	a pencil
un stylo	a pen
un lave-vaisselle	a dishwasher
le ménage	housework

Daily routine

Je me réveille	I wake up
Je me lève	I get up

Je me douche	I shower
Je me brosse les dents	I brush my teeth
Je m'habille	I get dressed
Je prends mon petit déjeuner	I have my breakfast
Je vais au travail	I go to work
Je rentre chez moi	I go home
Je dine en regardant la télé	I eat dinner watching TV

Weekend routine differences

Je fais la grasse matinée	I have a lie-in
Je sors avec mes amis	I go out with my friends
Je me détends	I relax
Je ne fais rien	I do nothing
Je passe la journée au lit	I spend the day in bed
Je le mérite!	I deserve it!

Jobs around the house

Je passe l'aspirateur	I vacuum
Je fais la vaisselle	I wash up *(vessels)*
Je lave la voiture	I wash the car *(lather)*
Je prépare le diner	I make dinner
Je ne fais rien	I don't do anything
Je ne fais pas beaucoup	I don't do much
Je n'ai pas le temps	I don't have the time

Town

tout ce dont j'ai besoin	everything I need

où on peut	where one can
Je vais au	I go to the (masc nouns)
Je suis allé **au**	I went to the (masc nouns)
Je vais **à la**	I go to the (fem nouns)
Je suis allé **à la**	I went to the (fem nouns)

Directions

tout droit	straight on
à droite	right
à gauche	left
aux feux	at the traffic lights
au carrefour	at the crossroads

Shopping

économiser / dépenser	to save / to spend
gaspiller	to waste
un portefeuille	wallet
les soldes	the sales
faire de la lèche vitrine	window shopping

Tickets

le guichet	ticket office
un billet simple	a single ticket
un billet aller-retour	a return ticket
c'est quel quai?	Which platform is it?
le consigne de bagages	left luggage

Road accidents

un pneu crevé	a flat tyre
un accident	an accident
un embouteillage	a traffic jam
en panne	broken down
la moteur	the engine
les urgences	the emergency services
les pompiers	the fire brigade
une ambulance	ambulance
un gendarme	policeman
un policier	policeman
heurter	to hit, crash into *(hurt!)*
le frein	brake
freiner	to brake
faire le plein	fill up with petrol
l'essence	petrol
la ceinture de sécurité	seat belt
la vitesse	speed
un amende	a fine
un témoin	a witness
le témoignage	testimony

Employment

le chômage	unemployment
travailler / bosser	to work
Il travaille comme	he works as a
un boulot, un métier, un emploi	job

bien payé	well-paid
à temps plein	full-time
à temps partiel	part-time
travail temporaire	temporary job
travail permanent	permanent job
il faut poser sa candidature	you have to apply
gagner un bon salaire	earn a good salary
beaucoup de chômage	high unemployment
un vendeur /vendeuse	salesperson
un / une professeur	teacher
un chauffeur	driver
un facteur	postman *(factory of letters)*
un médecin	doctor *(medicine)*
un pharmacien	chemist
un chirurgien	surgeon (shurgeon)
un comptable	accountant
un avocat / une avocate	lawyer *(advocate)*
un informaticien /-ienne	IT consultant
un / une secrétaire	secretary
un serveur / une serveuse	waiter
un ingénieur	engineer
un pompier	fireman *(pumps)*
un plombier	plumber
un gendarme	policeman
un infirmier / une infirmière	nurse *(infirmary)*
un coiffeur / -euse	hairdresser *(quiff)*
un photographe	photographer

un commerçant	shopkeeper
un ouvrier / une ouvrière	worker
un homme d'affaires	businessman
une femme au foyer	housewife

> *If you are talking about what you do for a job, **you don't need to say un or une** – so just say "je suis prof"*

Leisure

jouer au foot, rugby, cricket, hockey, tennis, golf etc	
jouer aux échecs	chess
jouer aux cartes	cards
jouer du piano	piano
jouer du violon	violin
jouer de la guitare	guitar
jouer de la clarinette	clarinet
jouer de la batterie	drums

Faire activities

faire du sport	do sport
faire du patinage	go skating *(pat ce)*
faire du vélo / cyclisme	go cycling
faire du VTT	go mountain biking
faire du judo / karaté	do judo, karate
faire du shopping	go shopping
faire du skate	go skateboarding
faire du ski	go skiing
faire du ski-nautique	go waterskiing

faire du jardinage	do the gardening
faire du bricolage	do DIY
faire du camping	go camping

faire de la – the beach scene

faire de la natation	go swimming
faire de la voile	go sailing (v upside down = sail)
faire de la planche à voile	windsurf *(plank with sail)*
faire de la plongée	go diving *(plunge)*
faire de la gymnastique	do gymnastics
faire de la danse	dance
faire de la musculation	do weight training

faire de l' – with vowels

faire de l'équitation	go horseriding
faire de l'athlétisme	do athletics
faire de l'escrime	do fencing *(scream!)*
faire de l'escalade	go climbing *(escalator)*
faire de l'alpinisme	go mountaineering *(alps)*

faire des – with plural activities

faire des promenades	go for walks
faire des randonnées	go for hikes

Other hobbies

la lecture	reading
lire	to read

aller à la pêche	to go fishing
collectionner	to collect
des timbres	stamps
dessiner	to draw
chanter	to sing
danser	to dance
tricoter	to knit

Cinema and TV

le dernier film que j'ai vu	the last film I saw
il s'agit de	it's about
je l'aime	I like it
je l'ai aimé	I liked it
ça me fait rire	it makes me laugh
passionnant	exciting
mon émission préférée	my favourite programme
je le trouve	I find it
un journal	newspaper
les dessins animés	cartoons
les actualités / les infos	the news
quotidien	daily
hebdomadaire	weekly
les feuilletons	soaps
les documentaires	documentaries
la téléréalité	reality TV
les jeux télévisés	game shows
la chaine	channel

l'écran	screen
les téléspectateurs	viewers
les auditeurs	listeners
les vedettes	film stars
la zapette	the remote control
les films romantiques	romantic films
les films d'action	action films
les films d'horreur	horror films
les films de guerre	war films
les films de science-fiction	sci fi films
les films d'aventures	adventure films
les films policiers	detective filims

On holiday

je suis allé	I went
j'ai passé	I spent (time)
quinze jours	a fortnight
au bord de la mer	by the sea
au camping	at the campsite
en montagne	in the mountains
nous avons logé	we stayed
dans un hôtel	in a hotel
dans une auberge	at a hostel
dans un appartement	in an apartment
dans une gite	in a gite
à la station balnéaire	at the holiday resort
à la station de ski	at the ski resort

louer	to hire
nous avons loué	we hired
les valises	suitcases
à l'étranger	abroad
j'ai perdu mon passeport	I lost my passport
retardé	delayed
le vol a été annulé	the flight was cancelled
on a perdu / raté l'avion	we missed the plane
il y avait trop de monde	it was too crowded
avec vue sur	with a view over
avec balcon	with a balcony
faire les valises	to pack suitcases
défaire les valises	to unpack
se bronzer	to sunbathe
se détendre	to relax
se reposer	to rest
se baigner	to swim
se souvenir de	to remember
visiter les musées	to visit the museums
prendre des photos	to take photos
gouter les plats régionaux	to sample local dishes
acheter des cadeaux	to buy presents
se faire de nouveaux amis	to make new friends
visiter les sites touristiques	to go sightseeing
Il a fait beau	the weather was good
Il a plu deux fois	it rained twice
une canicule	a heatwave

j'ai envie d'y retourner	I'd like to go back there
J'ai hate d'y aller	I can't wait to go there

Technology

mon portable	my mobile
mon ordinateur	my computer
je m'en sers pour	I use it to
envoyer des messages	to send messages
télécharger de la musique	to download music
accéder à l'internet	to go on the internet
rester à la page	to stay up to date
mettre à jour	to update
mon profil Facebook	my Facebook profile
rester en contact	to stay in touch
j'y suis accro	I'm addicted to it
scotché à l'écran	glued to the screen
je ne pourrais pas m'en passer	I couldn't do without it
le cyber-intimidation	cyber-bullying
les inconnus	strangers
le vol d'identité	identity theft
les sites de rencontre	chat rooms
les réseaux sociaux	social networks
rencontrer en ligne	to meet online
une tablette	tablet
planter	to crash

Environment

le changement climatique	climate change
la deforestation	deforestation
la pluie acide	acid rain
les tremblements de terre	earthquakes
l'énergie nucléaire	nuclear energy
les ressources naturelles	natural resources
en danger	in danger
les espaces verts	green spaces
la circulation	traffic
es embouteillages	traffic jams
les camions	lorries
les usines	factories
la sècheresse	drought
les inondations	floods (innundated)
les incendies	fires
les ordures / déchets	rubbish
la déchetterie	the tip
les poubelles	bins
le déboisement	deforestation
Je ferme les robinets	I turn the taps off
Pour économiser de l'eau	to save water
J'éteins les lumières	I turn off the lights
Je recycle les emballages	I recycle packaging
J'utilise	I use
les transports en commun	public transport
On doit / il faut	we must

Je vais continuer à	I am going to carry on
J'essaie de	I try to
Je fais des efforts pour	I make an effort to
protéger	to protect
éteindre	to switch off
trier	to sort out
les emballages	packaging
le verre	glass
le carton	cardboard
éviter	to avoid
voyager	to travel
manifester contre	to protest against

Social issues

la pauvreté	poverty
la faim	hunger
le terrorisme	terrorism
l'immigration	immigration
accueillir	to welcome
le racisme	racism
le chômage	unemployment
le taux de chômage	the rate of unemployment
est en hausse	is going up
le manque de	the lack of
l'obésité	obesity
la malbouffe	junk food
les sans-abris	the homeless

SDF (sans domicile fixe)	homeless
quelque chose d'utile	something useful
le travail bénévole	voluntary work
les organisations caritatives	charities

Weather terms

il fait un froid de canard	it's freezing
il pleut à verse	it's pouring
des averses	showers
le ciel est couvert	it is overcast *(covered)*
la météo	weather forecast
la chaleur	heat *(from chaud)*
la canicule	heatwave
le tonnerre	thunder *(a tonne in the air)*
un orage	storm *(rage)*
une tempete	storm
un éclair	flash of lightning
des éclaircies	sunny spells
frappé par la foudre	struck by lightning
dans le nord	in the north
dans le sud	in the south
dans l'est	in the east
dans l'ouest	in the west

Food

Un / une – if you eat / drink / want the whole thing

Most fruit is feminine, so imagine ladies eating fruit

une poire	pear
une pomme	apple
une banane	banana
une pêche	peach
une orange	orange
une mandarine	satsuma
une mangue	mango
une pastèque	watermelon
une cerise	cherry
une fraise	strawberry
une framboise	raspberry
une prune	plum (dried plums)

except

un ananas	a pineapple
un melon	a melon
un pamplemousse	a grapefruit
un abricot	an apricot

Steak with salad, followed by tart with ice cream and a cold drink FOR LADIES!

une salade	salad
une entrecôte	a steak
une tarte	a tart
une glace	an ice cream
une boisson	a drink
une limonade	a lemonade
une bière	a beer

Stodgy food and hot drinks FOR MEN!

un œuf	an egg
un croissant	a croissant
un biscuit	a biscuit
un gâteau	a cake
un sandwich	a sandwich
un chocolat chaud	a hot chocolate
un café	a coffee
un thé	a cup of tea
(except un jus d'orange	an orange juce)

"Du" - with masculine foods – think PICNIC

du pain	bread
du vin	wine
du boursin	(a type of french cheese)
du beurre	butter (bu- - er)
du fromage	cheese
du poulet	chicken
du jambon	ham
du canard	duck
du saucisson	sausage
du salami	salami
du bœuf	beef
du poisson	fish
du thon	tuna
du pâté	pâté
du gâteau	cake

du chocolat	chocolate
du sel	salt
du miel	honey
du sucre	sugar
du lait	milk

"De l'" if there is some of it and it starts with a vowel

de l'agneau	lamb
de l'eau	water

Plural food – if you eat / have lots, use "des"

des chips	crisps *(not chips!)*
des frites	chips
des escargots	snails
des céréales	cereal *(plural cereals)*
des pâtes	pasta *(plural pastas)*
des œufs	eggs *(the smell of eggs is – ugh)*
des légumes	vegetables
des pommes de terre	potatoes *(apples of the ground)*
des carottes	carrots
des petits pois	peas *(little peas)*
des haricots verts	green beans
des champignons	mushrooms *(champions)*
des oignons	onions
des choux de Bruxelles	brussels sprouts
des cerises	cherries
des fraises	strawberries

des framboises	raspberries
des raisins	grapes
des raisins secs	raisins *(dry grapes)*
des saucisses	sausages
des crêpes	pancakes
des bonbons	sweets
des fruits de mer	seafood
des moules	mussels
des crudités	raw vegetables

Au restaurant

j'ai faim	I'm hungry
un repas	meal
l'addition	bill
le plat du jour	dish of the day
les plats régionaux	local dishes
service compris	service included
un pourboire	tip
le serveur	waiter
Garçon!	waiter!
saignant	rare
à point	medium
bien cuit	well done
Bon appétit!	enjoy your meal!

The body

le bras   arm *(flex your biceps to show you are **bra**ve)*

la jambe	leg *(messy breakfast-eater drops **jam** on leg)*
la tête	head *(the accent is like a little hat on a head)*
la bouche	mouth
les oreilles	ears *(you can hear people shouting "**ooray!**")*
les épaules	shoulders *("hey Paul!" - slap his shoulder…)*
les genoux	knees
le nez	nose (horse with long nose says "**neigh**")
les dents	teeth *(think **dent**ist)*
le dos	back (**back door** sounds like back dos)
le ventre	stomach
la main	hand *(the **main thing** you need)*

Health

pour garder la forme	to keep fit
pour rester en bonne santé	to stay healthy
il faut / on doit	one must
manger sainement	to eat healthily
manger équilibré	eat a balanced diet
s'entrainer	to train
éviter le sucre	to avoid sugar
la malbouffe	junk food
bien que ce soit délicieux	although it's delicious
bouger	to move around
je fais un régime	I'm on a diet
il ne faut pas	one should not
ca fait grossir	it makes you fat
fumer	to smoke

se droguer	to take drugs
boire de l'alcool	to drink alcohol
on peut y devenir accro	you can get addicted
devenir	to become
déprimé	depressed
prévenir	to prevent
de graves maladies	serious illnesses
l'obésité	obesity
le sida	AIDS
de plus en plus de	more and more
le cancer de poumons	lung cancer
les crises cardiaques	heart attacks
des comprimés	pills
tousser	to cough
j'ai mal à la tête / au bras	my head / arm hurts
je me suis cassé la jambe	I broke my leg
un rhume / je suis enrhumé	a cold, I have a cold
la grippe	flu
être atteint de	to suffer from
la diabète	diabetes

Clothes

Je porte	I wear
Je mets	I put on
On doit porter	we have to wear
un uniforme	uniform
un pull	jumper *(pullover)*

un jean	jeans
un pantalon	trousers *(pants are long)*
un manteau	coat *(for a man, down to his toes)*
un chapeau	hat *(for a chap)*
un imperméable	raincoat *(impermeable)*
des gants	gloves *(same g as in English)*
bonnet	woolly hat
une robe	dress
une jupe	skirt
une chemise	shirt
une veste / un blouson	jacket *(false friend not vest!)*
une cravate	tie
une casque	helmet
une casquette	cap *(small helmet)*
une écharpe / un foulard	scarf
des chaussettes	socks *(you need a set)*
des chaussures	shoes *(you need to be sure of them)*
des bottes	boots
en coton, en laine, en soie, en cuir	cotton/wool/silk/leather

Accessories

des écouteurs	earphones *(listeners-écouter)*
des bijoux	jewellery
des lunettes	glasses *(little moons)*
du maquillage	make-up
un portable	mobile
un parapluie	umbrella *(for the pluie = rain)*

Colours

rouge	red
orange	orange
jaune	yellow
vert(e)	green
bleu(e)	blue
rose	pink
violet	purple
blanc (blanche)	white
noir(e)	black
marron (*no plural*)	brown (chestnut)
gris(e)	grey

Animals

un chien	a dog
un chat	a cat
un lapin	a rabbit
une vache	a cow
un cheval	a horse
un mouton	a sheep
un cochon	a pig
un cochon d'inde	a guinea pig
un serpent	a snake
un cheval (des chevaux)	a horse
un poisson	a fish

Time phrases

Il est neuf heures moins le quart	8.45
Il est deux heures et demie	2.30
Il est huit heures et quart	8.15
Il est trois heures vingt	3.20
Il est onze heures moins vingt	10.40
Il est minuit	midnight
à midi	at midday
hier	yesterday ("**hier**sterday")
demain	tomorrow
dernier	last
prochain	next *(ap**proaching**)*
la semaine dernière	last week *(note the e on both)*
l'année dernière	last year *(note the e on both)*
le weekend dernier	last weekend *(no e or accent)*
la semaine prochaine	next week *(e on both)*
l'année prochaine	next year *(e on both words)*
le weekend prochain	next weekend
avant de manger	before eating
en mangeant	while eating
après avoir mangé	after eating
de temps en temps / parfois	sometimes
tous les jours	every day
quand j'ai le temps	when I have time
chaque samedi / le samedi	every Saturday

Days of the week

lundi	Monday
mardi	Tuesday
mercredi	Wednesday
jeudi	Thursday
vendredi	Friday *(get the van ready)*
samedi	Saturday
dimanche	Sunday
lundi	on Monday
le lundi	on Mondays
le weekend	at the weekend

Months

janvier	January
février	February
mars	March
avril	April
mai	May
juin	June
juillet	July
aout	August
septembre	September
octobre	October
novembre	November
décembre	December

Seasons

au printemps	in Spring *("oh! it's Spring!")*
en été	in Summer
en automne	in Autumn
en hiver	in Winter
à Paques	at Easter
à Noël	at Christmas

Negative expressions

Je ne mange pas	I don't eat
Je ne mange jamais	I never eat
Je ne mange plus	I no longer eat
Je ne mange que	I only eat fruit
Je ne mange rien	I don't eat anything
Je ne vois personne	I don't see anyone
Personne ne le fait	Nobody does it

French things

un Parisien	person from Paris
le TGV	train grande vitesse (fast train)
le SNCF	French railway company
le VTT	mountain biking
les randonnées	hikes
la chasse	hunting
la boulangerie	baker's shop
la pâtisserie	cake shop
quinze jours	a fortnight

le lycée	sixth form college
un lycéen	a sixth former
un département	similar to a "county" of France
les escargots	snails

False friends (faux amis)

La location DOESN'T MEAN LOCATION

It means **rental**

Location (place) is endroit, lieu

La librairie DOESN'T MEAN LIBRARY

It means **bookshop**

A library is a "bibliothèque"

Personne DOESN'T ALWAYS MEAN person

It can mean **nobody**

To say a person it's "UNE personne", lots of people is "beaucoup de monde"

Passer les examens DOESN'T MEAN PASS EXAMS It means **to take exams**

To say pass you say "reussir" = succeed

Un roman DOESN'T MEAN ROMAN

It means **novel**

Roman in French is "romain"

La journée DOESN'T MEAN JOURNEY
It means **day**
A journey in French is "voyage"

Travailler DOESN'T MEAN TRAVEL
It means **to work**
Travel in French is "voyager"

Assister DOESN'T MEAN ASSIST
It means **to attend**
Assist in French is "aider"

Raisins DOESN'T MEAN RAISINS
It means **grapes**
Raisins are "raisins secs"

Sensible DOESN'T MEAN SENSIBLE
It means **sensitive**
Sensible is "raisonnable"

Most commonly forgotten words

sans	without
presque	almost *(nearly)*
devant	front of
souvent	often *(Sue visits often)*
avant	before *(in advance)*
derrière	behind

loin	far *(lions are far away)*
quel / quelle	which
qui	who
quand	when
combien de	how many
trop de	too many (with noun)
assez	quite (with adj)
surtout	especially, above all
déjà	already
heureusement	fortunately
malheureusement	unfortunately
toujours	always

(same number of syllables as the English)

tous les jours	every day

(same number of syllables as the English)

Numbers

un	1
deux	2
trois	3
quatre	4
cinq	5
six	6
sept	7
huit	8
neuf	9
dix	10

onze	11
douze	12
treize	13
quatorze	14
quinze	15
seize	16
dix-sept	17
dix-huit	18
dix-neuf	19
vingt	20
vingt-et-un etc	21
trente	30
quarante	40
cinquante	50
soixante	60
soixante-dix	70
quatre-vingt	80
quatre-vingt dix	90
cent	100

Countries and continents
Feminine – take "en"

La France	France
L'Angleterre	England
La Grande Bretagne	Great Britain
L'Ecosse	Scotland
L'Irlande	Ireland

L'Allemagne	Germany
L'Italie	Italy
La Belgique	Belgium
La Grèce	Greece
La Suède	Sweden
L'Europe	Europe
L'Amerique	America
L'Australie	Australia
L'Asie	Asia

Masculine – take "au"

Le Royaume Uni	UK
Le pays de Galles	Wales
Le Portugal	Portugal
Le Japon	Japan
Le Canada	Canada

Plural – take "aux"

Les Etats Unis	USA

Nationalities

anglais(e)	English
français(e)	French
espagnol(e)	Spanish
italien / italienne	Italian
portugais(e)	Portuguese
irlandais(e)	Irish

gallois(e)	Welsh
grec (grecque)	reek
hollandais(e)	Dutch
suédois(e)	Swedish
japonais(e)	Japanese
autrichien / autrichienne	Austrian
canadien / canadienne	Canadian
belge	Belgian
australien / australienne	Australian
européen(ne)	European
américain(e)	American

Thank you for purchasing this book. If you have any questions please do contact me through my website www.lucymartintuition.co.uk

You may also be interested in my other books, also available on Amazon:

How to Ace your French Oral

How to Ace your Spanish Oral

How to Ace your German Oral

Spanish vocabulary for GCSE

French Vocabulary for GCSE

Common Entrance French Handbook

Printed in Poland
by Amazon Fulfillment
Poland Sp. z o.o., Wrocław